A
Pocket
Guide
to
KAUA'I

text by **Curt Sanburn**
photography by **Douglas Peebles**

MUTUAL PUBLISHING

Library of Congress Catalog Card
Number: 00-100554

First Printing, August 2000
1 2 3 4 5 6 7 8 9

Design by Jane Hopkins

ISBN 1-56647-158-3

Mutual Publishing
1215 Center Street, Suite 210
Honolulu, Hawaii 96816
Telephone (808) 732-1709
Fax (808) 734-4094
e-mail: mutual@lava.net
www.mutualpublishing.com

Printed in Thailand

TABLE OF CONTENTS

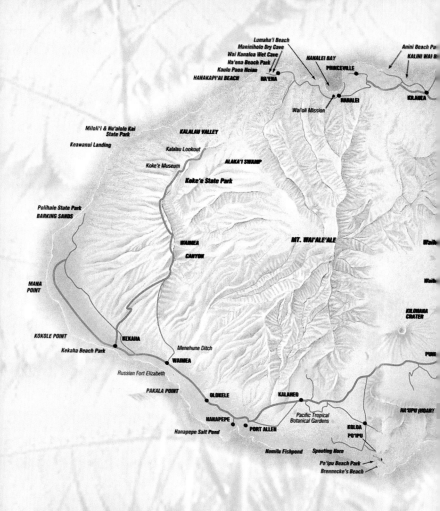

Lumaha'i Beach
Maniniholo Dry Cave
Wai Kanaloa Wet Cave
Ha'ena Beach Park
Kaulu Paoa Heiau
HANAKAPI'AI BEACH
HA'ENA

HANALEI BAY
PRINCEVILLE

Anini Beach Park
KALIHI WAI B

Wai'oli Mission
HANALEI

KILAUEA

Miloli'i & Nu'alolo Kai
State Park
Keawanui Landing

KALALAU VALLEY

Kalalau Lookout

Koke'e Museum

ALAKA'I SWAMP

Koke'e State Park

Polihale State Park
BARKING SANDS

WAIMEA
CANYON

MT. WAI'ALE'ALE

Waik

Waik

MANA
POINT

KILOHANA
CRATER

KOKOLE POINT

KEKAHA

Kekaha Beach Park

Menehune Ditch

WAIMEA

PUN

Russian Fort Elizabeth

PAKALA POINT

OLOKELE

KALAHEO

HA'UPU (HOARY)

HANAPEPE

Pacific Tropical
Botanical Gardens

KOLOA
PO'IPU

Hanapepe Salt Pond

PORT ALLEN

Nomilu Fishpond

Spouting Horn

Po'ipu Beach Park
Brennecke's Beach

KAUA'I
FACTS & FIGURES

County: Kaua'i; includes islands of Kaua'i and Ni'ihau

County seat: Lihue

Land area: Kaua'i 552 square miles (Ni'ihau 70 square miles)

Resident population: 56,603 (Kaua'i County, 1998)

Highest point: Kawaikini 5,243 feet

Shoreline: 90 miles

Extreme length and width: 33 miles by 25 miles

Average annual temperature in Lihue: 75.2°F

Highest recorded temperature: 95°F

Lowest recorded temperature (at sea level): 49°F; at Kokee (elevation 3,600 feet): 29°F

Average annual rainfall: Poipu, 35 inches; Lihue, 44 inches; Waialeale summit, 444 inches (the world record, 666 inches [55-plus feet], was set in 1982)

Chief industries: tourism, agriculture, construction

Energy sources: 52% from imported oil; balance from hydro-electricity and biomass fuels

Visitors per year: 1,040,340

Average visitors per day: 16,160

Hotel and condominium rental units: 6,969

Public and private golf courses: 8

Public tennis courts: 22

State Parks: 10 (1997)

County Parks: 64 (1998)

Recognized surfing sites: 330

A KAYAKER CRUISES ALONG KAUA'I'S SPECTACULAR NA PALI COAST.

INTRODUCTION

KAUA'I STANDS TO THIS day as a place apart. On most days, the sixty mile Ka'ie'ie Waho or Kaua'i Channel is wide enough that Kaua'i and its nearest neighbor, O'ahu, are out of sight of each other. Canoe paddlers in ancient days had to know their course between these islands, because often at mid-channel, neither island is visible. The island remained independent for fifteen years after Kamehameha the Great in 1795 completed his conquests of the Big Island, Maui, Moloka'i, Lana'i and O'ahu.

Archaeologists have found on Kaua'i mysterious stonework and implements never seen on the other

WAILUA ("TWO RIVERS") FALLS, FOUND ON KAUA'I'S EAST SIDE, DROPS 80-FEET AFTER HEAVY RAINS, CREATING A COLORFUL RAINBOW SYMBOLIC OF THE ISLAND'S BEAUTY.

THE USUALLY DESERTED BEACHES AND SHORELINES OF
KAUA'I SUGGEST THE ISLAND'S STATUS AS A PLACE APART,
AND JUST A BIT MORE REMOTE.

Hawaiian islands. Ancient Kaua'i and neighboring Ni'ihau had their own dialect of the Hawaiian language, using "t" and "r," in words where the windward islanders used "k" and "l." More than any other island, Kaua'i is steeped in lively storytelling, legends and myths. Every rock, peak and cave has ancient significance; gods and ghosts animate the remote beaches.

Kaua'i is the oldest Hawaiian island at roughly five billion years of age, five or six times the age of Hawai'i, the tallest and youngest of the islands, at the other end of the island chain. Frequent rains delivered by the northeast trade winds have eroded the island. Its alluvial plains are thick and rich, and its river valleys cut deep into the heart of the circular island's volcanic core.

The ancient Hawaiians may have been aware that their island would someday disappear. Legend says that a rock pinnacle at Ha'ena on Kaua'i's north shore will stand as long as Kaua'i does. When the rock falls, the island, too, will crumble. This is the succession of geological events for Hawaiian islands: first an island, then a rock, then an atoll, and finally a shoal of concern only to ships' navigators.

But Kaua'i's erosion has its positive side effects. One of Kaua'i's chief attractions is the drama it creates. Steep pinnacles and razorback ridges, remnant mountains draped in velvety folds, canyons whose rock walls reveal millions of years of multi-hued geology, and countless picture-perfect waterfalls—these are Kaua'i's treasures.

When the British explorer Captain James Cook landed at Waimea in January 1778, the *taro* farmers and fishermen of west Kaua'i thought his ships were floating islands covered with tall trees. They flung themselves to the ground when he or his men approached. They gave him water, pigs, bananas, yams and fish—everything he wanted. In Waimea Valley, Cook noted the neat geometry of the fields and the complex irrigation system. Expedition artist John Webber sketched the native *heiau* (temples) with their stone platforms, wooden towers and grimacing idols.

Across the island at Wailua, the island's *ali'i* (chiefs) and *kahuna* (priests) knew nothing of the momentous events in Waimea. They carried on as usual. They gathered taxes of food from the *maka'āinana* (commoners), feasted, played games, surfed, punished *kapu* (law) violators, had children and managed their vast estates. Their history was preserved in hours-long chants memorized by skilled court chanters who freely mixed history, legend and fantasy.

The chants told stories of giant warriors and petulant goddesses, of great ancestors and of creation itself (as in the famed creation chant called the *Kumulipo*); stories of voyages to and from Tahiti and the Marquesan islands; and marvelous tales of the *menehune*, a legendary race of spry mountain people who built huge walls, ditches, *heiau* and fishponds in the dark of night.

Anthropologists now say that there is no evidence that the *menehune* ever really existed. The legend, they believe, recalls the earliest Marquesan settlers on Kaua'i who were subsequently ruled by the later-arriving Tahitians. The scientists have yet to explain adequately the unique "*menehune*" stonework and engineering feats of ancient Kaua'i.

The legends remind everyone that there is more to Kaua'i's landscape than erosion. Stones are still piled in simple terraces where gods once danced. A sleeping giant dreams on a hilltop, while below him, in Kapa'a, families shop for frozen food. At Ha'ena, two stones are thought to be two legendary brothers who came ashore to die after a long sea voyage. Their sister is a rock out on the reef, visible at low tide.

Though its erosion continues unabated, Kaua'i remains a vibrant, formidable island. It urges you to listen to its stories and understand its past. In doing so, it asks you to protect its future so that the life of the island, the murmuring mysteries of its ancient valleys and cloud-shrouded mountains, will never erode.

A traveler wrote fifty years ago: "...most of all, Kauai remains in my memory an island of fable, so near its own myths that they materialize out of its rocks and hills and live in its shifting light."

✳   ✳   ✳   ✳
A SAILING CATAMARAN RESTS ON THE SHORE AT KALAPAKI BAY.

10   A POCKET GUIDE TO KAUA'I

A LITTLE OVER A CENTURY AGO, A POIGNANT HUMAN
DRAMA WAS PLAYED OUT HERE IN THE KOKE'E
MOUNTAINS, AMONG THE PRECIPITOUS CLIFFS ON THE
NA PALI COAST WHICH FORM KALALAU VALLEY.

VIGNETTES

The Story of Ko'olau of Kalalau

Ko'olau was a respected cowboy living in the 1890s with his wife and son in Kekaha, on the west side of Kaua'i. When it was discovered that he had leprosy (now known as Hansen's disease), he was told he must spend the rest of his life at the Kalaupapa quarantine settlement on Moloka'i island. He insisted that his wife and son come with him. The health authorities said no.

The west side of Kaua'i in 1893 was the scene of numerous leprosy-related incidents. Native Hawaiians, both young and old, were particularly susceptible to the disfiguring disease. Authorities felt obliged by medical practice at the time to isolate husbands from wives and children from parents, shipping the patients to Kalaupapa. Some villagers fled. Ko'olau and his wife and son took a treacherous trail from the Koke'e uplands into wide Kalalau Valley on the Na Pali coastline.

Later in 1893, deputy sheriff Louis Stolz appeared in the valley, looking for Ko'olau and others afflicted. Ko'olau, when told again that his wife and son could not accompany him, refused to leave. Sheriff Stolz left, but returned two weeks later, armed and with a posse. When he approached Ko'olau's hiding place, Ko'olau shot and killed him.

A few weeks later, soldiers of the Hawaiian provisional government sent a unit of soldiers with a howitzer. Ko'olau and his wife and son hid on a ledge on the face of a cliff in the back of the valley. In an exchange of gunfire, Ko'olau killed two soldiers. The family moved to a new hiding place. The soldiers raked the valley with howitzer blasts, but could not locate Koʻolau. The soldiers finally returned to Honolulu with fourteen of the valley's fugitives, but without Koʻolau, his wife Piʻilani, or their son, Kaleimanu. Friends brought them food and supplies, and they lived off the land, eating the shrimps and fishes of the stream, and fern shoots and bananas.

A FAMILY SITTING OUTSIDE THEIR HOME ON NIʻIHAU, CIRCA 1900. (PHOTO: AUCKLAND MUSEUM AND INSTITUTE)

✳   ✳   ✳

Kaleimanu, who was also infected, died in the valley. Months later, Koʻolau fell seriously ill and died as well, three years after their escape into Kalalau. Piʻilani buried him deep in the valley. She remained in Kalalau for several more weeks before returning to her home at Waimea.

Jack London told the story of Koʻolau in his *Stories of Hawaiʻi* (Mutual).

An 1873 description by Isabella Bird

"There were deep ravines, along which bright, fern-shrouded streams brawled among wild bananas, overarched by Eugenias, with their gory blossoms: walls of peaks, and broken precipices, grey ridges rising out the blue forest gloom, high mountains with mists wreathing their spiky summits, for a background: gleams of a distant silver sea: and the nearer many-tinted woods were not matted together in jungle fashion, but festooned and adorned with numberless lianas, and even the prostrate trunks of fallen trees took on new beauty from the exquisite ferns which covered them. Long cathedral aisles stretched away in far-off vistas, and so perfect at times was the Gothic illusion, that I found myself listening for anthems and the roll of organs. So cool and moist it was, and triumphantly redundant in vagaries of form and greenery, it was a forest of forests, and it became a necessity to return the next day and the next..."

The Casuarina, Kauaʻi's Beach Tree

"...there was one tree specially dedicated to Kauai, and it made both life and agriculture on the island possible. Wherever the powerful northeast trades whipped sea and salt air inland, killing everything that grew, men had planted the strange, silky, gray-green casuarina tree, known sometimes as the ironwood. Groves of this curious tree, covered with ten-inch needles and seed cones that resembled round buttons, stood along the shore and protected the island. The

The blue waters and striking cliffs of Kalalau Beach along the Na Pali coast.

foliage of the casuarina was not copious and to the stranger each tree looked so frail that it seemed about to die, but it possessed incredible powers of recuperation, and what it thrived on most was a harsh, salty trade wind that whipped its fragile needles into a frenzy and tore at its cherrybark trunk;

A HAUL CANE ROAD DIVERGES FROM KAUMUALI'I HIGHWAY IN THE WEST KAUA'I SUGAR FIELDS.

✶　　　✶　　　✶

for then the casuarina dug in and saved the island. The sea winds howled through its branches; its frail needles caught the salt; the force of the storm was broken and all who lived in the shadow of the casuarina tree lived securely."

—from the novel Hawaii
by James Michener

The Sugar Plantations

Sugar cane, a giant grass, was brought to Hawai'i as a food plant by the early Polynesian settlers, and was first planted commercially in 1802. But, the enterprise failed. The first commercial sugar plantation, Ladd & Co., was started at Koloa on Kaua'i in 1835.

The California Gold Rush and the American Civil War spurred the demand for sugar, and plantations sprang up on all the islands. A reciprocity treaty was arranged with the United States, dropping import duties on Hawaiian sugar. By 1890, Hawai'i was exporting 250 million pounds of sugar a year.

By purchase, marriage or legal maneuvering, vast tracts of arable land passed into non-Hawaiian hands and were consolidated for sugar cultivation. Mills were built and production improved. Engineers ran irrigation ditches and viaducts through mountain ranges to serve leeward plains. Railroads were strung across countless gullies and streams; harbors were blasted from lava shores. Corporate growers brought in expensive heavy equipment, which small farmers couldn't afford.

Labor was the planters' problem. Hawaiians, their population cut by disease, were generally neither available nor particularly interested in plantation work.

The plantation owners and the government began to look elsewhere for labor—to Germany and the Portuguese islands of Madeira and the Azores, then to China, Japan and the Philippines. Between 1852 and 1948, 350,000 contract workers arrived to work Hawai'i's twenty-seven plantations. When their contracts expired, some took their money and returned home, but many stayed. Their

JACK LONDON, AUTHOR OF *STORIES OF HAWAII*, WHEN HE VISITED HAWAI'I IN 1915.

IRONWOOD TREES, ALSO KNOWN AS CASUARINA TREES, OVERHANG THE SURF NEAR HANALEI ON KAUAI'I'S NORTH SHORE.

descendants have flourished, creating Hawai'i's great ethnic mix, which is sugar's lasting legacy.

Kaua'i's town of Kaumakani and the dirt roads of Makaweli are the best examples of plantation life as it was a century ago. Kekaha, with a no-nonsense layout and bulky mill, is less quaint. Parts of it resemble a mid-West rust-belt factory town that ended up on a beautiful tropical beach. Grove Farm Homestead Museum and the Kaua'i Museum, both in Lihue, are Kaua'i's two best sources for historical information about the industry that still exerts considerable influence on Hawai'i's landscape.

Ni'ihau

The island of Ni'ihau, seventeen miles west of Kaua'i, is an anomaly in modern Hawai'i. The next-to-the-smallest of the eight major Hawaiian islands, Ni'ihau is deliberately isolated from much Western influence. Its affairs, conducted in the Hawaiian language, are managed by a single, somewhat paternalistic *haole* family. About 225 Hawaiians and part-Hawaiians live in small houses provided by Ni'ihau Ranch. Rain is caught off the house roofs and collected in tanks for drinking water. There is no community electricity. Children use Hawaiian and English through the eighth grade, after which they go to high school on Kaua'i or to boarding schools in Honolulu.

With about twelve inches of rain a year, the dry pastureland supports 2,000 head of cattle, 3,000 wild turkeys and 12,000 sheep (raised for their wool). There are large numbers of destructive wild pigs, and in recent years, the ranch has established a hunting program.

✳   ✳   ✳   ✳

HE VIEW FROM THE KALALAU OVERLOOK FEATURES SHEER DROPS OF OVER 2,000 FEET TO THE VALLEY FLOOR, AND EXTREMELY NARROW RIDGES OFTEN ONLY A YARD WIDE AT THE TOP.

KNIFE-EDGED RIDGES AND PLUNGING CLIFFS DEFINE NA
PALI, KAUA'I'S NORTHWEST COAST.

NATURAL SPECTACLES

HAWAIIAN MYTHOLOGY NOTWITHSTANDING, the islands of Hawai'i were built by volcanic action. It began roughly seventy million years ago with what is now Meiji Seamount, and continues today on the Big Island at the southeastern end. A slow, steady northwestward drift of the Pacific plate over a volcanic "hot spot" accounts for the Hawaiian chain's linear track.

The typical young landform is a broadly rounded "shield" volcano, built up from the ocean floor to heights in excess of two miles above the sea by innumerable thin lava flows. Mauna Loa on the Big Island is a classic—and still active—shield volcano, rising gently to its 13,800-foot height above sea level (as high as most Rocky Mountain peaks).

On the eight major islands, it's easy to see the geological evolution of volcanic islands, from the broad, swelling shapes of intact young shield volcanoes on the Big Island and Maui to the heavily eroded, jagged topography of Kaua'i. Low-lying Ni'ihau island is almost completely worn down. Islands beyond it shrink steadily from oceanic rocks to atolls, and beyond the last dry land, Kure Atoll, there are the hundreds of miles of seamounts leading at last to Meiji.

The island of Kaua'i is the product of a single volcano whose oldest lavas are more than five million years old. Originally it was typically round in shape, rising to a central peak, which collapsed to form a huge caldera depression. The remains of the caldera

In one of Kaua'i's myriad interior streams, water flows into a pool shaded by ginger.

are found in the Alaka'i Swamp, a mile-high wetland. Rain runoff over millions of years carved great 2,500-foot-deep gorges in a radial pattern from the edges of the Alaka'i—Wainiha, Lumaha'i, Hanalei, Wailua, Hanapepe and Olokele streams—and along fault lines at Kalalau and Waimea Canyon.

Later, scores of volcanic vents created secondary features around the island, such as Poipu Crater and Pu'uhi Hill in Poipu, Kilohana Crater behind Lihue, and Crater Hill, a tuff cone near Kilauea Point.

Trade wind-driven waves have carved low sea cliffs along Kaua'i's northeast, windward coast, as well as on the spectacular Na Pali northwest coast. (Similar sea cliffs on Moloka'i island's north shore reach 3,000 feet, among the highest in the world.)

Hawai'i has few real "plains," mostly along the southwestern shores of O'ahu and Kaua'i. They are the result of sedimentation and coral-reef building, abetted by changes in sea level. Other land-shaping forces have been earthquakes, wind and, of course, man.

The Kilauea Point National Wildlife Refuge is home to several species of seabirds: shearwaters, boobies, albagross, great frigate birds and others.

The Na Pali coastline, with Kalalau Beach in the foreground, the Honopu arch beyond, and 'Awa'awaphui and Nualolo valleys in the distance.

The plentiful rainfall from Mt. Wai'ale'ale feeds hundreds of secluded mountain waterfalls.

Left: Much of Kaua'i's interior is composed of valleys like these which radiate out on all sides from the peak at the island's center. Such areas are accessible only by helicopter.

Following Page: Waimea Canyon, Hawai'i's "Grand Canyon," is 3,000 feet deep, a mile wide and ten miles long.

A SHADED WATERFALL IN HANALEI ILLUSTRATES THE BEAUTY THAT CAPTURED WRITER ISABELLA BIRD'S HEART.

TOURS

THE NORTH SHORE

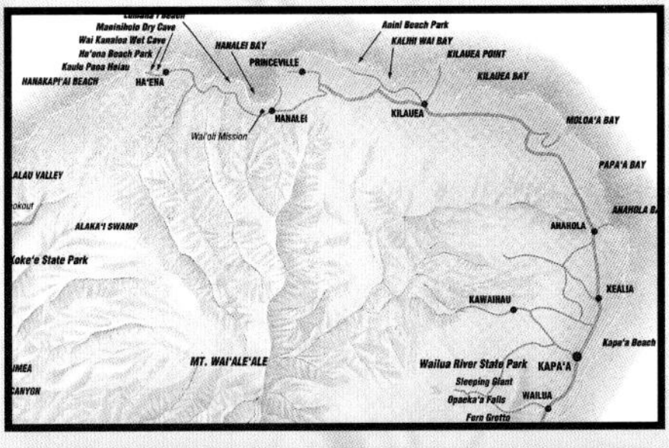

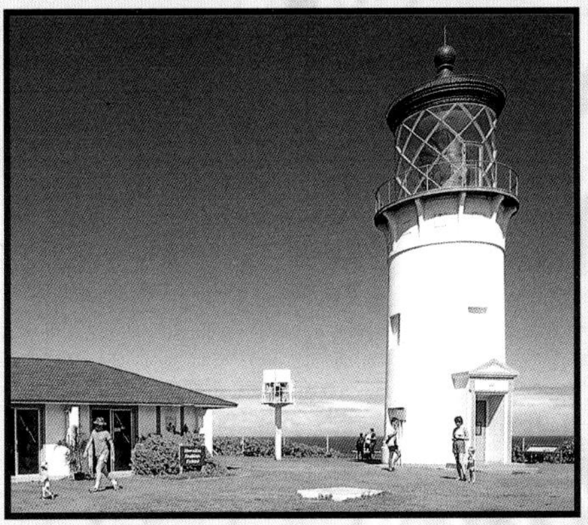

KILAUEA LIGHTHOUSE, NOW PART OF A NATIONAL WILDLIFE REFUGE.

FROM THE BAY AT Moloa'a on the east to the Na Pali cliffs on the west, Kaua'i's north shore is a splendid collection of cliffs, valleys, plateaus and beautiful shoreline, a fiercely defended region of old-fashioned agriculture, low-visibility wealth, great winter surf and abundant natural beauty.

Begin near the Meadow Gold diary where Kuhio Highway and Ko'olau Road meet, about seventeen miles north of Lihue. Ko'olau Road leads down to Moloa'a Bay, a small residential outpost facing a wild crescent of beach. The road is narrow and parking and beach access are limited. Park carefully, and follow the public right-of-way to the beach. For low-key waterfront living, Moloa'a is hard to beat. The bay, fringed with ironwoods, as are many of Kaua'i's northern beaches, is good for long walks and beachcombing.

In calm weather, swimming and snorkeling are excellent everywhere except right in the middle, where beach rock interrupts the sand.

Return to Kuhio Highway via Ko'olau Road and turn right. About three miles down the road is the old plantation town of Kilauea. The town has maintained a handsome collection of historic stone sugar plantation era buildings. Two interesting churches stand on Kolo Road. One is built in the shape of an octagon. A recommended stop in the town, which is just *makai* (seaward) of the main highway, is the landmark Kong Lung Store, now a gift and clothing boutique. The complex also includes a gourmet deli, a pizza place and an Italian restaurant set in a garden.

GUAVA TREES CAN BE FOUND ON THE *MAUKA* SIDE OF THE MAIN HIGHWAY.

✻ ✻ ✻

Lighthouse Road dead ends at Kilauea Lighthouse on the Kilauea peninsula.

The Kilauea Point National Wildlife Refuge, with 160 acres of sea cliffs, is home to several species of seabirds: shearwaters, boobies, albatrosses, great frigate birds and others. It's worth taking a look even if the gates are closed, since the views from the road end are remarkable. Entrance to the refuge is worth the admission fee; the views are superb, and the self-guided tour of the area is fascinating. There's a definite edge-of-the-world feeling here, especially in winter when the surf is raging. The old lighthouse is scenic, but has been supplanted by a modern light adjacent to it. Kilauea Point marks the northernmost extension of the main Hawaiian Islands.

On either side of Kilauea Point are substantial private houses belonging to film and sports figures.

To reach one of Hawai'i's most impressive hidden beaches, turn west onto Kauapea Road off Lighthouse Road between town and the lighthouse. Be alert. Particularly in wet weather you'll want to pass on this sight because of the treacherous access. Secret Beach is at the end of a steep, muddy path that starts between two fences, 0.3 mile from Lighthouse Road. The beach has a certain cachet as a summer nudist colony. During winter, sunbathers and beach both disappear. Nevertheless, at any time of the year it's a glorious spot and well worth the difficult walk.

On the *mauka*, or mountain, side of the main highway in Kilauea are the guava fields, Guava Kai Plantation, of Kilauea Agronomics. Look for signs to determine whether its visitor center is open.

West of Kilauea, Kuhio Highway dips gently into the wide gulch of the Kalihiwai River, which empties into the Pacific at Kalihiwai Bay. The first of two Kalihiwai roads leaves the highway just before you

Limahuli Garden, Ha'ena

Taro growing at Hanalei National Wildlife Refuge.

Harvesting the highly-nutritious *taro* roots and their edible leaves..

Coastline of the Princeville plateau, framed by *hala* trees.

cross the gulch and leads down to Kalihiwai Bay. The second Kalihiwai road, across the curving concrete bridge (check out the viewing area on the Kilauea side of the bridge), takes you along the shore to Anini Beach, where more movie stars have homes. Anini Beach Park, next along the shore, is popular for wind-surfing; across the road is a polo field.

WAIOLI MISSION HOUSE IN HANALEI, AN OLD MISSIONARY HOME, IS NOW A MUSEUM AND A DISTINCTIVE PIECE OF HAWAIIAN ARCHITECTURE

✳   ✳   ✳

Situated just beyond Kalihiwai is Princeville, the north shore's only true resort, with two golf courses—a 27-hole and an 18-hole and a permanent residential community. The master-planned development sprawls across old pastures above the sea and is the gateway to the north shore's legendary series of lush valleys and knife-edged ridges that begin at Hanalei and culminate in the Na Pali coast. The 252-room Princeville Resort is on the eastern headlands overlooking Hanalei Bay.

Right after the Princeville shopping center and the resort's main entrance, a lookout on the left side of the road shows green-on-green Hanalei Valley to its best advantage. *Taro* patches stretch deep into the valley, quilting the banks of the wide Hanalei River. Directly below the lookout is the Hanalei Bridge, the first of many one-lane bridges ahead. Over the years, these bridges have been the subject of controversy. Repeated proposals are floated to straighten and widen them to accommodate more traffic. Larger tour buses cannot squeeze through the narrow spans. So far, the quaint bridges have been defended suc-cessfully, in part because the larger tour buses cannot get through.

"See Hanalei and die" is as succinct as any advice ever given about Hanalei. The remark was quoted in 1873 by the English travel writer Isabella Bird, who went on to describe Hanalei's atmosphere and scenery as "so glorious that it was possible to think of nothing all day, but just allow oneself passively to drink in sensations of exquisite pleasure." It is intoxicating even now. Development has been kept to a whisper and the natural elements converge at Hanalei as at few other places in Hawai'i.

Past Hanalei Bridge, Hanalei Town announces itself with a few stores and restaurants, and a couple of understated shopping complexes, one of them a renovated old schoolhouse.

In the middle of downtown Hanalei (yes, this is it), Aku Road heads seaward to Weke Road, which follows the wide beachfront along Hanalei Bay. A right on Weke takes you past the

KAYAKING DOWN HANALEI RIVER.

THE CLASSIC TRUSSES OF THE HANALEI BRIDGE.

HANALEI PIER AND HANALEI BAY AT SUNSET.

grand, green-roofed Wilcox house (circa 1896) to Black Pot Beach Park and the Hanalei Pier. This beach, at the mouth of the Hanalei River, attracts surfers when winter waves sweep into the bay, peeling off in "sets" that can reach twenty-five feet in height. The end of the pier is a good place to count the waterfalls on Kaliko and Mamalahoa's slopes after a rain. The Hanalei River reaches the sea here, and is the site of a controversial commercial tour boat industry, which takes visitors on fishing trips, sailing cruses and motor tours down the Na Pali coastline.

Reversing direction on Weke Road, continue past some of Hawai'i's most beautiful beachfront residences to He'e Road and another beach access. This one, in the middle of the bay, offers excellent swimming (when the water is calm) and sunbathing (when the sun is out). During winter, great lines of surf crest and explode at "Pine Trees," just off the beach to the right of the parking area. From this point in the bay, there's fodder for a photo shoot in every direction. If the water is very calm, swim a little way for the full effect. You'll never forget it.

Kaua'i's missionary history is exquisitely preserved at Hanalei's

HISTORIC WAIOLI HUI'IA CHURCH.

✳   ✳   ✳

Waioli mission, located just beyond downtown Hanalei on Kuhio Highway. Broad lawns and ancient trees provide an idyllic setting for the 1912 Waioli Hui'ia Church, the 1841 Waioli Mission Hall and the 1837 Waioli mission house (now a museum) hidden behind the church in a gated garden. The grounds are always open and must be counted among Hawai'i's most magnificent residential gardens. With the help of one of the gardeners or a curator, you should be able to pick out a huge old breadfruit tree, several *kukui* trees, a massive *kamani*, several ancient *ti* plants, and a false *lehua* with delicate pink blossoms.

The steep-roofed Mission Hall once served as the mission church and was the center of Hanalei's social life. This building is a landmark in Hawaiian architecture. Its native grass-hut profile (the roof was originally thatched) was altered by the missionary builders with a second pitch to create eaves for a shady *lanai* (verandah). This distinctive double-pitch, now accepted as the traditional Hawaiian roofline, is used frequently in con-temporary Hawaiian architecture.

The Waioli Church Choir, the pride of Hanalei, sings old New the

THE CRESCENT SANDY SECTIONS OF LUMAHA'I BEACH ARE PERFECT FOR SUNBATHING.

England hymns in Hawaiian during Sunday services at the charming church.

The frequent one-lane bridges slow traffic to a very leisurely pace on the winding seven miles to the end of the road. Protocol is that if you are arriving at the bridge after the oncoming car, you stop and let that car through. If you're there first, cruise on through, but be alert. The other driver may be a tourist who doesn't know protocol.

HANALEI VALLEY, LUSH WITH GREEN PATCHES OF TARO, APPEARS CALM AND SERENE AS IT'S BATHED BY MID-DAY SUN.

✥　　✥　　✥

After leaving Hanalei, just around Makahoa Point, the road winds above much-photographed Lumahai Beach. Park just off the road near a sign marking the beach and hike down any of several steep, unmaintained paths. If the water is anything but flat calm, it's potentially dangerous for swimming, but sunbathing is hard to beat here. To get to the other end of the beach, continue driving until the highway returns to sea level and meets the Lumaha'i River. A dirt parking area, with an emergency telephone and caution signs, marks the western edge of Lumaha'i Beach.

The unprotected beach's scenery is matched by the number of drownings here.

Swimmers and strollers should always be cautious, especially during high surf. The Lumaha'i River, which empties into the ocean at the beach's western end, has never been diverted or tamed in any way, and is subject to dangerous flash floods during rainy weather.

The highway next enters Wainiha Valley, fronting Wainiha Bay and beach. A general store offers refreshments. Powerhouse Road, just beyond the Wainiha River, heads two miles into the lush valley at the base of the Wainiha *pali* (cliffs).

The agricultural scenery here (and the fact that this is the only paved road inland for miles) makes the short drive a worthwhile diversion. The roadside property here is private. Don't go wandering.

Ha'ena, a district that figures prominently in the the odyssey/romance/love triangle of the fire goddess Pele, her sister Hi'iaka, and the handsome chief Lohiau, is next. The *hula* platform where Pele first laid eyes on Lohiau and where she chanted for him still stands overlooking Ke'e Beach (pronounced kay-ay). The three caves in the neighborhood are the result of Pele's looking for a place to settle down with her chosen husband. (She craved

PRINCEVILLE PLATEAU AT HANALEI WAS NAMED FOR PRINCE ALBERT, THE ONLY CHILD OF KING ALEXANDER LIHOLIHO (KAMEHAMEHA IV) AND QUEEN EMMA, WHO DIED WHILE STILL YOUNG. TODAY IT IS HOME TO LOW-RISE CONDOS AND A GOLF COURSE WITH SPECTACULAR VIEWS.

warmth of a fire pit. Finding none on Kaua'i, she finally settled at Kilauea volcano on the Big Island.) Near the end of the saga, Pele sends her sister Hi'iaka to fetch Lohiau, and they fall in love, angering Pele. After several battles and scenes that include death and resurrection, the pair finally escapes Pele's vengeance, to live happily ever after. Naturally.

"Tunnels" beach near Ha'ena Point is a spectacular and relatively safe place for swimming, reef fishing and snorkeling, except when surf is high. The big outer reef protects the shore waters and produces "clean" waves much appreciated by surfers and windsurfers. But swimmers must always be aware of possible strong currents, even when it is calm.

Further on, the Maniniholo Dry Cave looks ready to swallow Haena Beach Park, a popular camping spot.

The end of Kuhio Highway comes suddenly at Ke'e. The road ends because the countryside gets so vertical nobody could figure out how to drive any farther. It is a scene of dizzying splendor: streams to beaches to mountainside pinnacles to pounding surf to foliage to flowers, clouds, and mysterious caves. The tour ends here for the less adventuresome, but the Na Pali Coast begins for hikers, kayakers and others.

❋ ❋ ❋ ❋

KE'E BEACH PEEKS THROUGH A TANGLE OF PALM TREES

COCONUT PALMS, WHILE NOT NATIVE TO HAWAI'I, ARRIVED WITH
THE EARLIEST POLYNESIAN SETTLERS. A CENTURY AGO, WHEN THERE
WAS A MARKET FOR COPRA (THE DRIED MEAT OF THE COCONUT),
PALMS WERE PLANTED IN LARGE PLANTATIONS. THE BEST REMAINING
EXAMPLES OF THESE PLANTATIONS ARE FOUND AT WAIMEA, WAILUA
AND WAIPOULI.

THE EAST SIDE

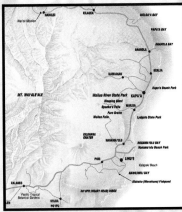

THE WELL-WATERED, GENTLY rolling eastern coast has always been Kaua'i's most populous district. The towns of Anahola, Kapa'a, Wailua and Lihue share a generally sandy windward shore and a wide coastal plain suitable for rapid growth.

At the midpoint of the corridor is Wailua, Kaua'i's most historic district, where the two forks of the Wailua River descend from rain-soaked Wai'ale'ale and join to meet the sea. The beloved silhouette of the Sleeping Giant on Nounou Ridge presides over the green shores and valleys of Wailua, the exclusive domain of the island's ruling ali'i (hereditary leaders), until the death in 1855 of Kaua'i's last queen, Deborah Kapule. Wailua's ancient legends and stories underscore its fame not only in Hawai'i, but also among the Tahitians and Marquesans who

TOUR BOAT TO FERN GROTTO PLIES THE RIVER.

✵   ✵   ✵   ✵   ✵

traveled back and forth to Wailua's rich shores a thousand years ago.

Several *heiau* (temples), sacred stones and other artifacts and sites, comprising the so-called Wailua Complex, remain and are worth a careful look. South of the river mouth stands an old coconut grove shading scattered large stones. These are the much-diminished remains of Hikinaakala Heiau, a massive rectangular temple built in 1200 A.D. Nearby is an unprepossessing stone rectangle, Pu'uhonua Hauola, once one of the island's two *pu'uhonua* (places of refuge).

Death was a common punishment for *kapu* (taboo) violators and defeated warriors. Hawaiian tradition, however, had a remarkable route to absolution. If the condemned could evade capture and reach the threshold of a *pu'uhonua*, he might be absolved by the resident *kahuna pule* (priest). The fugitive then was free to resume his normal life.

To reach this shoreline, especially beautiful at sunrise and sunset, use the Lydgate State Park access road south of the Kaua'i Resort on Kuhio Highway. The hotel crowds the archaeological site and adjacent beach park.

Across the highway from the hotel is the Wailua River Marina and Smith's

ENTERTAINMENT AT THE FERN GROTTO.

✻ ✻ ✻

Tropical Paradise, a botanical theme park and garden.

Tour boats to the Fern Grotto, a moss and fern-festooned cave upriver, leave the marina on the half-hour on a ninety-minute cruise.

Directly north of the Wailua Bridge, busy Kuamo'o Road (Route 580) takes you into inland Wailua. The two large stones of Holoholoku, Pohaku Ho'ohanau and Pohaku Piko are a quarter-mile up Kuamo'o Road on the left, tucked under the cliffside where the ridge begins its rise. The stones mark the birthing site of Kaua'i's ancient *ali'i*. At birth, the child's umbilical cord was wedged into the Pohaku Piko (*pohaku* means stone, *piko* means navel). It was propitious if the cord was not eaten by rats. If it was eaten, the child might become a thief. A dog's bones, buried under the flat rock at the entrance of the birthing place, ensured that the site was *kapu*.

Past the stones, Kuamo'o Road climbs the ridge that overlooks the river. At the top, Poliahu Heiau commands views of Wailua, the Wailua River and Kaua'i's peaceable windward kingdom. Poliahu is Kaua'i's largest *heiau* which, legends say, *menehune* helped to build. Its situation reminds the visitor

WAILUA FALLS, A 200-FOOT
DOUBLE WATERFALL, IS WORTH
VISITING.

THE WATERS OF 'OPAEKA'A FALLS
EVENTUALLY FLOW INTO THE WAILUA
RIVER.

WAIPOULI'S COCONUT PLANTATION, WITH THE SLEEPING GIANT IN BACKGROUND.

of a Greek temple. Poliahu Heiau was used for human sacrifice, and it is thought that its rituals were held simultaneously with similar rites in another large *heiau* visible near the shore.

THE KAPAʻA SLEEPING GIANT FORMS AN IMPRESSIVE BACKGROUND FOR SUGAR CANE FIELDS.

＊ ＊ ＊

The short dirt road to the *heiau* continues seaward to some large "bell stones" at the very edge of the escarpment. Supposedly, these stones, when struck, issued a resounding tone, announcing the birth of a male *aliʻi*.

Across Kuamoʻo Road is the parking area for ʻOpaekaʻa Falls, a scenic stop popular among photographers.

Kuamoʻo Road continues inland for several miles. The thickly settled Wailua Homesteads is home to many of Kauaʻi's permanent residents, who value the area's cool air, moderate rains and rural feeling. The winding road reaches an effective end for rental cars as it fords a stream at the state Division of Forestry and Wildlife's Keahua Arboretum. This park has no explanatory signs and no labeled trees, but the paths through its cleared meadows are pretty. The up-close views into Waiʻaleʻale's eastern ramparts or south to Kilohana Crater are grand.

Backtracking on Kuamoʻo Road, turn north onto Kamalu Road (Route 580), which dead-ends into Olohena Road, for a back-country drive into the former plantation town of Kapaʻa. You'll pass back of the Sleeping Giant. A thirty-minute hike to the giant's chin and forehead gives great views of the entire east coast of Kauaʻi.

Olohena Road returns to the coast in "downtown" Kapaʻa, flanking Kuhio Highway for three blocks. There's new life in the old wooden buildings, particularly at night, with several excellent bars and restaurants.

The *makai* sections of southern Kapaʻa and neighboring Waipouli are busy resort areas, as well as shopping and dining centers. The narrow beaches all along this coast, from the Wailua River north to Kealia, are marginal for swimming, but rather beautiful and wild in the prevailing northeast trade winds. The backshore is fringed by ironwoods, *kamani* and coconut trees as well as several hotels and many condominium complexes. The shallow, patchy coral reefs, beachrock, seawalls and canal outfalls are primarily the domain of fishermen and beachcombers, although families enjoy Kapaʻa Beach Park, particularly at its southern end. The most obvious scenery in the neighborhood is the huge coconut grove along the highway at Waipouli, beneath which was built the Coconut

WAILUA RIVER VALLEY CURVES INTO KAUAʻIʻS INTERIOR.

Plantation resort, including several hotels, a condominium project and the attractive Coconut Plantation Market Place shopping arcade. The grove was planted as a commercial venture for the making of copra, the dried meat of the coconut, which yields an oil that remains useful in soaps, suntan oils and food.

North of Kapa'a, a pinnacled ridge guards the coast, marking the farthest reach of Kaua'i's windward kingdom. Anahola settlement and romantic Anahola Bay lie directly beneath the green landmark, which some say has King Kong's profile. Kaua'i was the jungle scenery for the most recent remake of the movie, *King Kong.*

To reach Anahola Bay and its peaceful beach park, travel north on Kuhio Highway, then right on Anahola Road to the park at the south end of the bay. This offers what is considered to be the safest swimming on the windward side. Across the bay, the beach stretches northward with a soft fringe of ironwoods. If you seek solitude, you can walk the mile-long stretch, but you may have to ford the mouth of Anahola Stream. Otherwise, you'll have to drive back to the main highway and continue north across

KAUA'I LAGOON GOLF COURSE OVERLOOKS NAWILIWILI BAY.

✳   ✳   ✳

Anahola Stream to Aliomanu Road. A pretty drive brings you to the long, empty beach again, where the ironwoods provide plenty of backshore shade.

Swimmers should be cautious here, however, especially during periods of high surf.

At the south end of the windward shore, complementing the Anahola ridge to the north, Haupu Ridge is a prominent coastal feature. The seaward edge drops precipitously to the water at Nawiliwili Harbor, Kaua'i's chief port, situated six miles seaward of Lihue, Kaua'i's county seat and major town.

On your drive into Lihue from the north, you will want to take a side trip to Wailua Falls via Ma'alo Road. At the end of the road, the 200-foot double waterfall is visible from behind a white retaining fence. Stay behind the fence. There have been numerous deaths and injuries here to incautious people who ventured to the area atop the falls, or onto the steep valley's walls. If you go back down the road to the previous wide spot in the road, there's a marginal way down to the stream and the base of the falls.

If there has been rain, stay on the pavement and just enjoy the thunderous power of the falls.

Alekoko Fishpond, also called the Menehune Fishpond, along the Huleia River.

Lihue and neighboring Nawiliwili, Hanamaulu and Puhi are linked in a pattern of new roads, new shopping areas, a bigger airport, shrinking cane fields, and an ambitious program of new suburban homes. It's an easy place to get lost. But, before you do, find the downtown district along Rice and Umi streets, a few blocks *makai* of the intersection of Kuhio Highway (Route 56) and the island's southern highway, Kaumuali'i Highway (Route 50). Here you'll find two important sources of information about the island: the Kaua'i Museum's easy history lessons on Rice

Street, and travel tips at the Kaua'i office of the Hawai'i Visitors Bureau, in the Lihue Plaza Building on Umi Street.

The Grove Farm Homestead Museum on Nawiliwili Road is a wonderful introduction to plantation life as it was lived by the *kama'aina* Wilcox family and their employees from 1864 until the 1940s. The gracious old compound is open for small group tours, only on certain days, and by advance reservation only. But for anyone interested in the history of Hawai'i, it's worth it.

Picturesque Nawiliwili Harbor, at the foot of Nawiliwili Road, is a

KILOHANA, A RESTORED PLANTATION MANAGER'S HOME, LIES SOUTH OF LIHUE.

commercial harbor, a resort area, and a quiet backwater all at once.

The Kauai Marriott Hotel and Kauai Lagoons Golf Course front the white sands of Kalapaki Beach, one of Kaua'i's popular and safe beaches, overlooking Nawiliwili Harbor.

Public access to the beach is via Nawiliwili Beach Park, or through the resort's public parking lot.

A casual drive past the harbor, turning right after the little one-lane concrete bridge, takes you to the overlook of Alekoko or Menehune Fishpond on Huleia Stream, whose wetland qualities have made it part of a national wildlife refuge. In former times, charming Niumalu was an important Hawaiian settlement; now it is a beach park with a small boat harbor at the mouth of Huleia and Puali streams.

A little south of Lihue on Kaumuali'i Highway are the Kukui Grove Center, a large mall featuring restaurants, shops, a pharmacy and more, and Kilohana, a grand plantation house built in 1935 and renovated as a restaurant, museum and collection of small shops.

TREE TUNNEL ON MALUHIA ROAD, LEADING TO KOLOA AND POIPU.

THE SOUTH SHORE

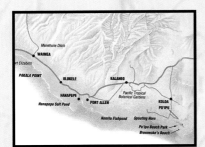

PLANTING SUGAR CANE NEAR KOLOA.

✳   ✳   ✳   ✳   ✳

SUNNY BEACHES AND POSH hotels characterize the narrow, very specific south shore. The resorts at Poipu, the popular beaches from Lawai Kai to Mahaulepu, and the upland towns of Koloa, Lawai and Kalaheo are in the district.

Traffic from Lihue to Kaua'i's south shore and extreme west side is via Kaumuali'i Highway (Route 50), to Knudsen Gap, the only level route. Just beyond the gap, Maluhia Road branches off to the left (seaward) through a splendid tree tunnel to the communities of Koloa and Poipu.

Poipu beaches have everything —sun, calm blue water, white sand, colorful reefs and facilities—for enjoying it all. Poipu ranges from the Fantasy Island glamour of Lawai Kai to Hawaiian legend-laden Mahaulepu. In between, sand crescents serve a string of beach hotels, condominiums, a few private homes, and public beach parks. Kona (southern) storms are rare, giving Poipu the island's safest beaches year-round. Protected from the usual trade winds by the bulk of the central mountain massif, the leeward water is also exceedingly clear, making this coast by far the island's best for snorkeling and scuba diving.

In Koloa Town, Maluhia Road jogs to the right and left, and resumes its southerly route as Poipu Road. Near the shore the entrances to the Waikomo Villas and the Kiahuna Plantation announce your arrival in resort territory. A string of resort properties on white sand beaches ends at the Sheraton Kauai and Hyatt Regency Kauai, the area's centerpiece hotels.

A right turn from Poipu Road to Ho'owili Road leads to Poipu Beach Park and Brennecke's Beach.

Return to Poipu Road and continue eastward past the condos on

GENTLE SURF AT POIPU BEACH.

✳   ✳   ✳

Makahuena Point to the Hyatt at Keoneloa or Shipwreck Beach. There is a public parking lot for beach access at the far end of the hotel property.

Except for its golf course, the green-roofed Hyatt Regency Kauai is the last sign of "civilization." Poipu Road becomes a privately owned dirt road used to haul sugar cane. The privacy protects Mahaulepu, a series of shallow bays, pocket beaches and rocky, sun-baked bluffs all the way to the Haupu cliffs and one of Kaua'i's key undeveloped coastal areas. Sand dunes in the area hide vulnerable Hawaiian gravesites as well as the fossil remains of extinct Hawaiian wildlife, preserved by the dry, salty climate. Development pressure on Mahaulepu looms as Kaua'i's next big land-use struggle.

Return to the west end of Poipu Road, past the shopping center at Kiahuna Village, to a left turn on Lawai Road. This is Poipu's other half.

Beside the road, Kuhio Park marks the birthplace of Prince Jonah Kuhio Kalaniana'ole, the Territory of Hawai'i's delegate in the U.S. Congress for twenty years. Hoai Bay was an important Hawaiian settlement. There are many stony rem-nants of it in the park, including the little pool that was once a working fishpond.

Kukuiula Harbor is the focus of the south shore's growing ocean recreation industry. Several commercial sailing tours, deep-water fishing and dive operators make Kukuiula their home port. The bay also has a small park and a faithful cadre of shore fishermen. This whole area was devastated by Hurricane Iwa in 1982 and Hurricane Iniki in 1992. Houses, moorings, even the road disappeared. It is a tribute to the people of Kaua'i that restoration has been so complete.

Near the end of Lawai Road is Spouting Horn Park, a series of lava tubes on a rocky shelf through which the ocean surge forces water and air, creating a miniature, musical version of Old Faithful. Naturally, the effect is most spectacular (up to sixty feet high) when the seas are roughest.

Koloa Town must be noted for its history. It had the first sugar plantation on the island in 1835. An old mill

Horesback tour at CJM Country Stables near Poipu.

The old sugar village of Numila, named for the new mill built there at the turn of the century.

foundation and smokestacks are visible in town, alongside a memorial to the many ethnic groups that played a role in the history of sugar cane.

One of the prettiest sites in Koloa is Saint Raphael's Church, on Weliweli Road east of town. Its dirt driveway is marked. The stark architecture of the 1854 red-roofed stucco church creates an austere, yet beautiful, scene in the middle of a sugar cane field. A few outbuildings, a rude lawn, a cemetery and a low lava-rock wall complete the picture. This church epitomizes the history of the Portuguese plantation workers who came to south Kauaʻi in the late-nineteenth century and stayed to prosper.

Inland from Koloa, via Koloa Road (Route 530), are three of Kauaʻi's most beautiful public gardens. The most important and impressive is the National Tropical Botanical Garden and the adjoining Allerton Gardens at Lawai, a sprawling valley with its own private bay. The gardens get their name from Robert Allerton and his adopted son, John Gregg Allerton, who are major contributors to the establishment of the national garden. The grounds are full of tropical specimens collected from around the world, as well as working horticultural nurseries, elegant formal gardens, even the restored cottage of Queen Emma, who honeymooned here and lived in the valley for several years after the death of her husband, Kamehameha IV, in 1870. Tours are by reservation only. There is an admission fee.

On top the hill in Kalaheo, just beyond Lawai on Kaumualiʻi Highway, is Kukuiolono Park and Golf Course, another private estate-turned-public park. It has a nine-hole golf course, Japanese gardens, with a "stream" of white rocks running through them, and several sacred stones. The stones were collected and brought to Kukuiolono by the land's former owner, sugar cane planter Walter McBryde. To reach the park, turn toward the ocean on Papalina Road, through the town of Kalaheo, to the park. The views are grand from the gazebo at the park's summit.

Completing the trio is Olu Pua Gardens, a paid visitor attraction, just west of Kalaheo on Kaumuali'i Highway. Bamboo forests, palm collections, banks of heliconia, view-filled meadows and grizzled Norfolk Island pines punctuate this luxurious old estate. A sign on Kaumuali'i Highway marks the short drive to the visitor center, where guided tours of the property begin. Once the home of the Kaua'i Pineapple Plantation manager, the main house at Olu Pua is a gorgeous example of work by C. W. Dickey, the architect responsible for many of Hawai'i's most distinguished homes in the 1920s and 1930s.

BICYCLING ON LAWAI ROAD NEAR KUKUI'ULA HARBOR.

Lilies in a pond at Allerton Gardens in Lawai.

A sunny day at Poipu Beach.

A LOW, GENTLE SURF AND A SCATTERING OF CLOUDS THAT OFFER SHADE BUT NOT RAIN STORMS ARE CHARACTERISTIC OF MANY OF KAUA'I'S LEEWARD BEACHES.

THE WEST SIDE

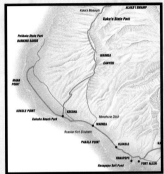

DRY SKIES, ENDLESS BEACHES and local flavor characterize Kaua'i's west side, where the old plantation towns of Hanapepe, Waimea and Kekaha barely disturb the cane fields. Inland, Waimea Canyon and the Kokee highlands add depth to the west side picture.

The West Side can be said to begin just beyond Kalaheo on Kaumuali'i Highway, where an overlook peers into Hanapepe Valley's ancient gorge. *Taro* has been growing in this valley for a thousand years. The dry, red canyon walls come as a bit of a shock for they are the first indication that not all of Kaua'i is a lush garden.

The three seaside towns that define the west side seem to have little in common except their serene detachment from modern life. Hanapepe is rustic, a bit ramshackle and full of productive farmers and hotel workers who commute to Poipu. Waimea is proud of its historic Russian fort, an elegant bank building, its one-

A WEST KAUA'I CATTLEMAN'S DECORATION.

✵   ✵   ✵   ✵   ✵

time commercial importance, and a statue of English explorer Captain James Cook dominating the New England-style town green. (Cook made his first Hawai'i landing here in 1778.)

Kekaha, three miles further west, is a no-nonsense, working sugar plantation town laid out for efficiency along a flat, hot, dry beach. At sunset, Kekaha is transformed, perhaps because the orange sun picks up some of the reds of the plantation dust, or perhaps just because sunset gives us new perspective.

Everyone's favorite main street is in Hanapepe, a right turn off the main highway as it descends the valley wall toward the Hanapepe River. The

THE OLD WAIMEA SWINGING BRIDGE WAS DESTROYED IN HURRICANE INIKI, BUT HAS BEEN REBUILT.

✳   ✳   ✳

old buildings lining the unimproved boulevard look like the Wild West, complete with a pool hall.

Hanapepe calls for free-form exploring. Drive up Awawa Road into the agricultural heartland, or down Puolo Street to the funky beach park. Route 543 heads *makai* from the highway at the west edge of town to Salt Pond Beach Park. Next to it are the famous salt ponds of Hanapepe, where Hawaiians continue to harvest their favorite sea salt from the red-earth beds.

Westward from Hanapepe, the landscape begins to broaden into a sea of sugar cane extending from the Makaweli highlands to the sea. Most of the land within view (56,000 acres, plus the 46,000-acre island of Ni'ihau, visible across Kaulakahi Channel to the west) is owned by the Gay and Robinson Plantation.

Less than three miles beyond Hanapepe, Kaumakani Avenue (the only "avenue" on Kaua'i) is visible on the left. Two old-fashioned lamp posts and a stately double row of monkey-pod and other trees line this impressive old driveway to the Olokele mill, offering a wonderful look at the sugar economy's former importance. Comfortable residences, a fine little office building, and the mill itself (still working) line the avenue. Older guides will refer to this as Olokele Sugar Company, but it has been absorbed by neighbor Gay & Robinson. The village of Kaumakani is changing. Its elementary school has closed and students moved to Ele'ele School, but plantation housing remains, along with the old grocery store, and the new Ni'ihau Helicopters office. This mostly intact and self-contained of Kaua'i's working sugar plantation towns does not offer tours. Snoop around, anyway.

Driving back toward Waimea, you'll pass the guarded entrances to Makaweli (or Pakala), the Robinson family headquarters.

On your left just before you reach the Waimea River bridge, Waimea's Fort Elisabeth, built circa 1816, was the result of a plan by a German adventurer to

Hawaiian saltmaker at the historic Hanapepe Salt Ponds.

The false-front buildings and shaded sidewalks of Hanapepe date from the early part of the twentieth century, and have a frontier style common to many old plantation towns.

Kayakers prepare to race in Hanapepe, with a rainbow in the distance.

take control of Kaua'i in the name of Tsar Alexander of Russia. The fort was named for the tsarina. The plan failed, but the star-shaped fort walls remain on the eastern headlands at La'auokala Point, guarding Waimea Bay and the mouth of the Waimea River. The clearly marked site, now a State park, has been somewhat restored. The walk inside the tumbled walls is kind of eerie.

MYSTERIOUS MENEHUNE DITCH, WHOSE ORIGINS ARE UNKNOWN.

✳   ✳   ✳

The fort looks out on the spot where English explorer Captain James Cook first set foot in the Hawaiian Islands on January 21, 1778. His two ships anchored off Waimea for two days, provisioning and exploring the prosperous village and valley at Waimea. When a storm threatened their anchorage, they sailed across the channel to Ni'ihau Island, where a group went ashore for two days. The expedition then sailed for the North American coast.

Probably the greatest mystery in Hawaiian archaeology is the "Menehune Ditch," reached by turning right off Kuhio Highway at Menehune Road, next to the police station in Waimea Town. Follow the road about a mile and pull over when you have river to your right and cliff to your left. A bronze tablet in the roadside cliff gives some background about the low rock wall running about sixty feet along the inland side of the road. Notice the regular finish of the stones, the clean, square cuts, the several notched joints. It is the only example known of Hawaiian cut stone-work.

Knowledgeable historians and archaeologists say this curiously fine stonework is the remnant of an irrigation ditch that once ran for miles. Early European visitors attest that the ditch was already there when they first explored Kaua'i in the late eighteenth century. Who built the Menehune Ditch? Legend has it that the *menehune* did, but there is no evidence that these little, supernaturally strong people actually existed, much less carved these elegant stones. If you look closely in the rubble on the opposite side of the road, you'll see several of the carved blocks tumbled at the river's edge.

Using irrigation systems such as the Menehune Ditch, the valley at Waimea has been cultivated, especially with *taro*, for hundreds of years. In 1787, an English sea captain, George Dixon, noted that the valley was "entirely planted with taro; and these plantations are laid out with a great deal of judgement... they would reflect credit even on a British husbandman." Waimea Town is at the foot of the Waimea Canyon Drive (Route 550), one of two

Aerial view of Waimea River, with Waimea town (left) and the Russian Fort (right).

Weathered goat skull graces a rock at midstream.

FOR A DIFFERENT EXPERIENCE, STAY AT WAIMEA
PLANTATION COTTAGES AND REVISIT THE PLANTATION DAYS
OF OLD IN THEIR REFURBISHED CAMP HOMES.

roads up the spectacular canyon rim to the Kokee highlands. (The other is Kokee Road via Kekaha.) You'll remain at sea level to the end of the road in Polihale, then return to Kekaha for the upland tour.

The beaches from Waimea to Polihale start out dark gray at Lucy Wright Beach Park near the mouth of the Waimea River, and get whiter as you travel west. One of the longest stretches of sand in the state starts at Kikiaola Boat Harbor, near Kekaha, and finishes fifteen miles away at Polihale Beach and the Na Pali coast's impassable ramparts. It's a beach lover's dream, the whole stretch, with western exposure toward the sunset and the islands of Lehua and Ni'ihau on the horizon.

Just west of Waimea, tucked in a huge coconut grove along a sandy beach, is one of Hawai'i's newest and most unconventional resorts, Waimea Plantation Cottages. Most of the cottages are transplanted camp homes from the old plantation camps at Mana, Kekaha and Waimea. Cleaned up with new bathrooms, fresh paint and wicker and koa furniture, they sit very casually under the tall trees, fronting a sand beach, amid green lawns and traditional plantation home landscaping. Very unusual, very real, and the only hotel between Poipu and Koke'e.

The most popular sections include Kekaha Beach Park, the beach at the Pacific Missile Range Facility at Mana (PMRF), and Polihale itself. The high-tech PMRF's beach is normally accessible via the main entrance near the end of Kaumuali'i Highway. The security desk will want to see your driver's license, car registration and no-fault insurance card or car rental agreement. Ask about water conditions, which are often dangerous here.

Civilization and Kaumuali'i Highway end at Mana. From there to the Polihale cliffs is nothing but sugar cane, bad roads and beach. Signs direct traffic to Polihale Beach, indisputably worth the five dusty miles of rutted cane-haul road. Polihale, like Kilauea Lighthouse and Ke'e Beach, is extremely beautiful. The huge cliffs, beach and surf are awesome and unforgettable—especially at sunset.

The peak of Mount Wai'ale'ale is almost always shrouded in clouds, very rarely visible. Its wealth of water keeps the entire island green and often sends sudden, violent rainstorms surging over Waimea Canyon.

WAIMEA CANYON & KOKE'E

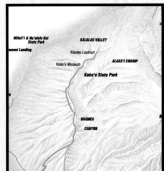

This tour, while not a long one, is presented as a separate excursion so that you can plan a full day up here if you have any interest in hiking any of the scenic trails in Koke'e State Park. The hikes are highly recommended. Waimea Canyon Drive and the companion Koke'e Road join seven miles up the mountain. They continue as Koke'e Road the remaining thirteen miles up the broad slope of the Waimea Canyon's west rim and then through the Koke'e State Park forests to an elevation of 4,000 feet at the Kalalau Valley lookouts. The 4,300-acre upland park is headquarters for Kaua'i's wild and largely inaccessible highland plateau, from which all of the island's dramatic valleys, cliffs and gorges descend. Waimea Canyon has its source in the Alaka'i Swamp, where annual rainfall averages 450 inches. The swamp is some eight miles long, with its wettest spot at the eastern end, the area known as Wai'ale'ale. From the swamp the waters spill down to form innumerable waterfalls, and to feed the bigger Kaua'i rivers, including

KOKE'E NATIONAL HISTORY MUSEUM NEAR THE KOKE'E STATE PARK HEADQUARTERS IS A TROVE OF INFORMATION ABOUT THE ISLAND.

❈   ❈   ❈   ❈   ❈

Bright red ʻohiʻa-lehua blossoms stand like sentinels at Kalalau Lookout, situated at 4,000 feet in the cool Kokeʻe Mountains.

Wainiha, Lumaha'i, Hanalei, Wailua, Hanapepe and Waimea.

On your way to the top, be sure to stop at the marked scenic lookouts for the dramatic views of Waimea Canyon. Hawai'i's "Grand Canyon," the gorge is 3,000 feet deep, a mile wide and ten miles long.

At the park headquarters is a large lawn surrounded by simple, lodge-style buildings, including the state-owned Koke'e Lodge. The Lodge has twelve cabins with kitchens that can be rented, but reservations must be made well in advance. These cozy cabins with fireplaces are popular with residents and *akamai* (smart) visitors. The Lodge is the only place up there for breakfast and lunch. Check in at park headquarters, which is the small building nearest the road, or at the Koke'e Natural History Museum, on the far side of the Lodge, for information on trails and hiking conditions. Please protect the wild fowl that have free run of the park. These birds look like particularly colorful chickens, but they carry the blood of the jungle fowl brought to Hawai'i by the early Polynesian settlers.

TWO GOATS AT REST OVERLOOK WAIMEA CANYON.

Papa'a Beach

Secluded Papa'a Beach is protected by reefs on Kaua'i's eastern shore.

BEACHES

KAUA'I HAS THE MOST diverse and abundant assortment of beaches in Hawai'i. The island's 113-mile perimeter includes about fifty miles of beach.

Uninterrupted stretches of sand gird the low-lying southwest corner and fringe the bays of the north shore. If crowds gather at Poipu with its scalloped lagoons, or at Kalapaki's busy harborfront, it's because they are great beaches. On the other hand, some hard-to-reach "secret" coves, familiar only to local fishermen or to well-guided visitors, are usually empty.

To generalize a little, the beaches on the north shore are the most scenic. Green mountains rise behind them, and in the winter, pounding surf can roll in. Those on the eastern shore are sometimes cloudy, and the onshore tradewinds often blow over them. South side and west-facing beaches are the sunniest. The east side beaches provide sunrise views, and some of the most stunning sunsets are seen from Hanapepe and beyond.

(Papa'a Beach is a small crescent of sand protected by reefs on the east side, typical of several such strands between the Wailua River and Kilauea.)

All shorelines and beaches in the State of Hawai'i are public up to the vegetation line. Beachfront-resort and residential-community development must provide public access to the shore. Rights-of-way from public roads are marked (some better than others). Where the land is privately owned and there are no paved roads, however, access to a beach may require hiking along the shore or approaching by boat. Kaua'i's

characteristic problem is that private sugar plantation lands often lie between the highway and the sea. Each situation is different, but the trend is toward government-enforced access and more cooperative landowners.

Kipu Kai

Kipu Kai valley, just south of Nawiliwili Bay, is a private, working cattle ranch, but its late owner's will provides that on the death of his heirs, the beach and valley will be given to the state for use as a public park. Diving and sailing cruises sometimes visit the beach.

HANALEI

THE RUGGED NORTH SHORE BEACHES OF THE HANALEI REGION ARE SOMETIMES HAZARDOUS WHEN THE HUGE WINTER SURF POUNDS THE SHORELINE, BUT IN SUMMER THEY OFFER SOME OF THE BEST SWIMMING AND SNORKELING SPOTS ON THE ISLAND. SUNSETS ARE STUNNING HERE, AGAINST THE BACKDROP OF THE STEEP MOUNTAINS THAT FORM THE BEGINNING OF THE NA PALI COSTLINE.

POIPU

FOUR CRESCENTS OF SAND SEPARATED BY LOW LAVA-ROCK POINTS CONSTITUTE THE BEACHES AT POIPU. THE FOCUS OF KAUA'I'S MOST INTENSIVE RESORT DEVELOPMENT, POIPU IS NO HIDEAWAY. ITS BEACHES ARE CONSISTENTLY SUNNY AND SAFE (EXCEPT DURING HIGH SURF SEASON), AND THE ROCKY POINTS OFFER OUTSTANDING SNORKELING. POIPU WAS COMPLETELY REARRANGED BY HURRICANES IWA AND INIKI. THE BEACHES HAVE RESTORED THEMSELVES TO THEIR FULL GLORY, BUT THE STORM STORIES—AND THE COMMENT, "YOU SHUDDA SEEN IT BEFORE!"—ARE UNABATED.

KALIHIWAI BAY

AN IDYLLIC IRONWOOD-SHADED SPOT AT THE MOUTH OF THE KALIHIWAI RIVER, THIS WIDE, SANDY BAY BEACH IS EASY TO GET TO AND IS RARELY CROWDED. WHEN THE WINTER WAVES ARE UP, SURFERS PADDLE INTO THE SHADOW OF THE HIGH CLIFF ON THE EAST SIDE OF THE BAY, WHERE THE WAVES PEEL RIGHT AGAINST THE ROCKS. THE BEACH ITSELF SLOPES GENTLY AND THE BREAKERS ROLL OVER A SANDY BOTTOM. BEHIND THE BEACH, THE RIVER MEANDERS INTO THE LEFT SIDE OF THE BAY THROUGH A THICKET OF IRONWOODS.

KE'E BEACH

THIS POPULAR, END-OF-THE-ROAD BEACH (PRONOUNCED "KAY-AY") IS A SORT OF BOOKEND FOR THE NA PALI SEA CLIFFS. THE OTHER BOOKEND IS POLIHALE, FIFTEEN MILES TO THE WEST. BOTH BEACHES ARE TRANSCENDANT PLACES. THERE IS GOOD SUMMER SWIMMING AND SNORKELING IN THE WIDE LAGOON RIGHT OFF THE BEACH, BUT BE CAREFUL OF THE CURRENT THAT RUNS OUT OF THE CHANNEL INTO DEEPER WATER. DURING PERIODS OF HIGH WINTER SURF, STAY ON THE SAND!

ADVENTURES

WHETHER YOU PLAN NOTHING more demanding than snorkeling off your hotel beach and touring botanical gardens, or you long for something ambitious such as hiking, scuba diving, horseback riding, windsurfing, penetrating the Alakai Swamp or kayaking the Na Pali coast, Kaua'i has it all arranged.

Warm air and high-energy wind and sea conditions make Hawai'i a natural spot for the athletic, particularly for those who love the ocean. The islands have become one of the world's great water sports centers. International athletes flock to Hawai'i for surf contests, long-distance swimming races, deep-sea fishing tournaments, inter-island canoe and kayak competitions, windsurfing championships, and trans-Pacific yacht races. On shore, brawny triathletes, daring hang-gliders and mud-stained hikers carry the "just do it" ethos to new extremes, 365 days a year.

A RURAL KAUA'I HOME SPORTS EVIDENCE OF THE RESIDENTS' INTEREST IN HORSES.

OPPOSITE PAGE: AN INFLATABLE TOUR BOAT CRUISES ALONG THE RUGGED CLIFFS OF NA PALI AT HONOPU BEACH.

Snorkeling

Kaua'i is a little far north for great coral displays, but that doesn't inhibit the fish and shouldn't interfere with your enjoyment of the velvety blue depths of a south shore cove. Their configuration and openness to the wind and sea affects the diving characteristics of certain areas, and the east coast and many west-facing beaches frequently have less than first-rate snorkeling.

A HIKING TRAIL AT THE RIM OF WAIMEA CANYON.

✳   ✳   ✳

Except during high surf season, the best snorkeling and diving is in the Koloa-Poipu-Mahaulepu area on the south shore. The north shore, on the other hand, is good for snorkeling only in summer, when the water can be glassy.

The most common sightings in Hawai'i's waters are endless numbers and varieties of reef fish—tangs, triggerfish, trumpetfish, stickfish, wrasses, Moorish idols, blowfish, mullets and, yes, the *humuhumunukunukuapua'a*, Hawai'i's unofficial state fish. Scattered across the sea floor are sea cucumbers, glossy black spiny sea urchins (don't touch!), bright red "pencil" urchins, and black urchins that try to camouflage themselves by attaching bits of coral and debris to their stubbly outer shells. In deeper sand-bottom areas you'll see *ulua*, barracuda, green sea turtles, reef sharks and, if you're lucky, Hawaiian monk seals and manta rays.

Hiking

Kaua'i's forests, valleys and cliff-sides include some Eden-like places that must be experienced to be believed. Virtually nothing dangerous exists in the Hawaiian forests, except an occasional wild pig—no poisonous snakes, no leeches, and few nasty insects, except mosquitoes.

The most famous hiking trip on Kaua'i is over the Kalalau Trail, an ancient, often muddy, and sometimes mildly hazardous eleven-mile path that hugs cliffs and zigzags in and out of the Na Pali coast's near-vertical valley mouths to the big one, Kalalau. The strenuous two-day hike into and back out of Kalalau requires some advance planning and provisions. Get an overnight camping permit from the State Parks Division (274-3344).

To get a taste of Na Pali without committing two days to it, you can limit yourself to the two-mile (each way) hike from the trailhead at Ke'e Beach to Hanakapia'i.

Complementing the Kalalau Trail's straight-forward hiking is the tangle of twenty-seven high-country trails centered on Koke'e and Waimea

THE VIEW DOWN THE SPINE OF THE HAUPU RANGE, WITH NAWILIWILI BAY AT THE UPPER LEFT.

KAYAKERS EXPLORE THE ROCKY NA PALI COAST AND ITS SURPRISE WATERFALLS.

Canyon. Their characters range from the desert-dry gorges in the canyon to the bizarre bogs and miniature trees of Alaka'i Swamp and the heavily-forested, precipitous lookouts above the Na Pali coast. Brisk, cool air, fast-moving clouds, and stunning peek-a-boo vistas make this roof of Kaua'i wonderfully invigorating. Koke'e State Park headquarters, next to Koke'e Lodge, is the best place to orient yourself for an all-day or half-day hike. The Park rangers can make recommendations, provide maps and let you know about trail conditions.

NATIVE WHITE HIBISCUS AT LIMAHULI GARDENS, A LUSH SANCTUARY OFFERING RARE AND NATIVE HAWAIIAN PLANTS, LOCATED ABOVE KE'E BEACH.

✳   ✳   ✳

A Walk in a Garden

Scientists now estimate that about 400 species of plants gained a footing in Hawai'i in the ten million years between its fiery creation and the arrival of the first Polynesians. These plants arrived at a rate of one species every 20,000 years. Over the centuries they evolved into about 2,700 different native plants, many found nowhere else and many now extinct.

The Polynesians brought the plants they needed to survive: coconut, *ti*, banana, *taro*, *kukui* and sugar cane among them. Still later, Westerners introduced their own ornamentals and crop plants, including scores now regarded as weeds. Some of Hawai'i's most characteristic plants today are actually not native —pineapple, orchid, anthurium, torch ginger, fragrant plumeria. But they all flourish in the well-watered volcanic soil, and Hawai'i, now more that ever before, is a garden.

And Kaua'i... well, Kaua'i is the garden of gardens. The old, heavily-eroded red earth island stands alone in the Pacific, bearing the full brunt of the moist northeast trade winds that flow relatively smoothly across Kaua'i's "streamlined" mass, dropping moisture equitably on fields, forests and valleys. That's why Kaua'i is so green.

Among Kaua'i's most elaborate gardens are the National Tropical Botanical Garden and the Allerton Estate at Lawai, which can be viewed in a three-hour walking tour (reservations and admission fee required, phone 332-7361), the mature residential-style gardens at Waioli Mission House in Hanalei (free), the Olu Pua estate near Kalaheo (admission fee) and Kukuiolono Park and Japanese garden in Kalaheo (free). There are all sorts of other possibilities, ranging from the casual displays at Keahua Arboretum above Wailua Homesteads to the high-tech resort

VIBRANT GINGER BLOSSOMS WHICH GROW WILD IN RAINFORESTS AND ALONG TRAILS.

THE ROMANTIC HANAKĀPĪʻAI VALLEY WATERFALL ATTRACTS VISITORS AND HONEYMOONERS FROM ALL OVER THE WORLD.

landscaping at the Kauai Marriott Hotel outside Lihue and the Hyatt Regency Kauai at Poipu. The hike to Hanakapia'i is a walk in nature's own garden and Kokee is itself a forest garden, dotted with Japanese Sugi pines, Norfolk Island pines, *koa* trees, rare *iliau* plants and *'ohi'a-lehua*. The remote Alaka'i Swamp is a bonsai garden, a forest of dwarf trees trying to survive on a terra that's so wet it's no longer firma.

A RELAXING DAY AT THE BEACH.

✢   ✢   ✢

For true connoisseurs, the National Tropical Botanical Garden at Lawai maintains a satellite garden on 1,000 acres in Limahuli Valley on the north shore, near Ha'ena. Once the private preserve of the *kama'aina* Rice family, Limahuli is a lush sanctuary for many labeled rare and native Hawaiian plant species, as well as introduced tropicals that love the very wet conditions here. The setting of the garden, perched in a narrow, high valley above Ke'e Beach, is sublime.

Horseback Riding

Three commercial stables can provide leisurely horseback touring of Kaua'i's meadows and valleys. And they provide views of dramatically different parts of the island: the North Shore, the South Shore, and the West Side.

Viewing Na Pali

If you're not interested in hiking into Kalalau and you can't quite justify the Na Pali helicopter tours, but you like the water and don't mind getting wet, join six or eight fellow travelers for a cruise along the awesome Na Pali coast in an inflatable boat. Your neck will ache from craning it upward at the impossible cliffs and velvet pinnacles. Along the way, depending on sea conditions, your "rubber ducky" may cruise into a narrow sea cave, then slosh out again, your heart in your mouth. All the while, you're surrounded by impossibly blue water in which a dolphin or a sea turtle, or even a whale, might appear at any time. Take an all-day summer tour and you'll land for snorkeling and exploring at isolated Nualolo Kai or Miloli'i beaches.

Sea tours of the Na Pali coastline are among Kaua'i's most popular and rewarding adventures, although residents are concerned about the growing pressure on the river's ecosystem from commercial tours based at the mouth of the Hanalei River.

There are also kayaking, fishing and sailing tours from Hanalei, and motorized tours from the West Side of Kaua'i at Port Allen and Kikiaola Small Boat Harbor.

LEFT: RIDERS RE-LIVE OLD KAUA'I COWBOY DAYS AT PRINCEVILLE RANCH.

BELOW: CAMARADERIE IS AN IMPORTANT PART OF HAWAIIAN OUTRIGGER CANOEING. HERE, A PADDLER LASHES THE OUTRIGGER WITH HEAVY COTTON CORD.

A WIDE HELICOPTER WINDOW PROVIDES A BREATHTAKING VIEW OF THE NA PALI COASTLINE.

Kayaking

Hot on the heels of the nation-wide fitness craze, the sport of kayaking has taken off as a whole-grain way to stay healthy. Kayak designs have proliferated to the point where the nomenclature is hard to follow. What is an ocean kayak? A sea ski? A surf ski? What is an "enclosed" kayak? What, in heaven's name, is a "royak"? In any case, kayaking is a peaceful, healthy and ecologically sound way to journey up one of Kaua'i's mellow rivers, or to power across a windy stretch of water. (Every year over a hundred international competitors race across the exceedingly rough and wild thirty-two-mile Ka'iwi Channel from the island of Moloka'i to Honolulu.)

A number of firms rent kayaks and safety gear, and can point you to quiet rivers and rugged ocean shores.

This kayaker takes a leisurely tour following the Na Pali Coast.

TRADITIONAL STOREFRONTS MAINTAIN THE
CHARACTER OF KOLOA TOWN.

CIVILIZATION

NOT SO LONG AGO, Kaua'i meant sugar plantations, few tourists and a low-key approach to everything except pig hunting. The Coco Palms Resort, the old Waiohai Hotel, the Hanalei Plantation and the Kaua'i Surf were the only substantial hostelries.

Early in the 1980s everything changed. Between 1983 and 1988, the island's average daily visitor count rose from 8,000 to 16,000. And as the numbers increased, Kaua'i added things for visitors to do, as well as to spend money on.

Shopping

Kaua'i has two big shopping centers. Kukui Grove Center at the corner of Kaumuali'i Highway and Nawiliwili Road in Lihue is the island's big mall. The tourist-oriented Marketplace at Coconut Plantation is a quaint shopping center with a sugar plantation theme.

GOOD FOOD WITH AN INTERNATIONAL THEME IS SERVED FROM A MOBILE KITCHEN.

It's at the south end of the picturesque coconut grove on Kuhio Highway between Kapa'a and Wailua. More than seventy shops, two cinemas, and several bars and restaurants make up the outdoor, low-rise complex.

Most of Kaua'i's quality boutique shops are in little shopping villages, hotel arcades or restored mansions. Kilohana, a 1930s

A COCONUT HAT AND A PLUMERIA LEI MAKE A PICTURE OF HAWAI'I THAT IS RECOGNIZED AROUND THE WORLD.

✳   ✳   ✳

plantation manor house on Kaumuali'i Highway near Lihue, has been transformed into an historical complex of art, craft and clothing shops, and a restaurant. And now and then there's polo on the front lawn.

Princeville Center and the Kiahuna Shopping Village, fine-tuned retail centers on opposite ends of the island, serve the busy resort traffic at Princeville and Poipu, respectively. They are worth visiting for beach gear, tee-shirts, resort logo-wear, sundries, frozen yogurt, pizza and big-ticket impulse items like art, jewelry and real estate.

The Kong Lung Store in Kilauea sells a little of everything: fine silk and linen, men's and women's resort wear, $300 panama hats, furniture, lighting fixtures (including Noguchi rice-paper lamps), and gifts. Next to Kong Lung are a gourmet grocery, a fine little gallery selling landscape and floral paintings inspired by Kaua'i's natural glamor, and a nifty indoor/outdoor Italian restaurant. Just down Kolo Road is the Hawaiian Art Museum and Bookstore, a low-key place to buy good local music tapes, books and some crafts.

Both the Kaua'i Museum in Lihue and the Koke'e Natural History Museum sell books, maps, crafts and other material with Hawaiian themes.

Restaurants

The most publicized eating places are the hotel dining rooms. Some are on the fancy side, but there are plenty of excellent casual steak and seafood eateries. Increasingly, you needn't drive far to find an excellent meal. Do you prefer seafood? Italian? Polynesian-flavored fine cuisine? Great burgers? Western-atmosphere steakhouses? There's this and more.

Lu'au

Poi, the Hawaiians' traditional staple starch, should be tried at least once, preferably at a full-blown *lu'au* feast. The idea of eating *poi* is similar to the starches you're more familiar with. Like potatoes and rice, you generally eat it along with something more flavorful.

LEFT: A ROADSIDE CASUAL RESTAURANT AT ANAHOLA.

BELOW: HISTORIC COMMERICAL BUILDINGS IN KOLOA TOWN HAVE BEEN RESTORED TO HOUSE OFFICES AND SHOPS.

AN INVITING VIEW OF THE HANALEI MOUNTAINS FROM THE POOL AT THE PRINCEVILLE RESORT.

(Although connoisseurs like nothing better than a bowl of *poi* all by itself, eaten with the fingers.) You'll find plenty of flavor at a *lu'au*. Try the dried beef (*pipikaula*), pork roasted in a pit (*kalua* pig), pork and butterfish steamed in *ti*-leaf wrapping (*lau lau*), salmon mixed with onion and tomato (*lomilomi* salmon), coconut pudding (*haupia*) and a bunch of side dishes.

Several hotels stage *lu'au* that usually include Hawaiian or Polynesian shows.

Best, however, is a real neighborhood celebratory *lu'au*. Community or church groups put them on occasionally, sometimes as fundraisers. Ask your concierge or look in the newspaper.

Nightlife

On Kaua'i, go to bed early. The best things happen during the day and are free, so it makes sense to get plenty of sleep. There is little to stay up late for, anyhow.

But for insomniacs and chronic party animals, there are several nightclubs around the island, generally in hotels. The island also attracts a range of visiting entertainers, who appear in auditoriums, hotel ballrooms, or even in stadiums. To experience the very best Hawaiian music, dance and feasting, you'll have to do some homework. Check the newspaper's entertainment calendar for community *lu'au* and special musical celebrations open to the public. Also, look for school concerts, fundraiser *hula* competitions and more. Ask your hotel concierge to help you. Call the mayor's office where people usually know what's going on, and can help you dig into the island's deeply musical community.

Most of all, and best of all: relax, relax, relax. That seems to be the reason a Paradise like Kaua'i was created in the first place.

❊   ❊   ❊   ❊

Breathtaking sunset bathes Hanalei Bay in brilliant oranges and reds—a perfect ending to a perfect day.

THE SYMBOL OF A TRAVELER'S DREAMS—AN EMPTY
HAMMOCK SHADED BY RUSTLING PALM LEAVES,
LOOKING OUT ON A LOVELY STRETCH OF SAND
WITH BEAUTIFUL BLUE WATERS BEYOND. LIE DOWN
AND RELAX...